Easy Carrot Cookbook

50 Delicious Carrot Recipes: Simple
Methods and Techniques for Cooking
with Carrots

By
BookSumo Press

Published by
http://www.booksumo.com

Table of Contents

Lovely
Curry Soup

🥣 Prep Time: 10 mins
🕐 Total Time: 35 mins

Servings per Recipe: 8
Calories	161 kcal
Fat	11.1 g
Carbohydrates	15.4g
Protein	2.7 g
Cholesterol	0 mg
Sodium	317 mg

Ingredients

4 cups vegetable broth
2 teaspoons curry powder
1 teaspoon ground cumin
1/2 teaspoon ground cinnamon
1/2 teaspoon ground ginger

2 pounds carrots, peeled and chopped
1 (14 ounce) can coconut milk
14 ounces water
1 teaspoon chopped fresh cilantro (optional)

Directions

1. Get your broth boiling in a saucepan with a medium level of heat then combine in the carrots, ginger, curry powder, cinnamon, and cumin.
2. Stir everything then set the set to low and let the soup gently boil for 22 mins. Stir the stir about 5 mins.
3. Take out your carrots from the liquid and place them into a food processor and add some of the broth into the processor as well so that the container is about halfway full. Puree everything carefully and work in batches to get all the carrots pureed. You may want to strain everything into a 2nd pot to separate the carrots from the broth.
4. Put the pureed carrots back into the broth and combine in the water and coconut milk. And get the soup gently boiling again. Once the mix is simmering add in the cilantro and stir everything.
5. Shut the heat and let the soup cool for about 15 mins.
6. Enjoy.

COCONUT
Toffee Trifle

Prep Time: 20 mins
Total Time: 2 hrs

Servings per Recipe: 16
Calories	520 kcal
Fat	35.4 g
Carbohydrates	44.7g
Protein	7.3 g
Cholesterol	87 mg
Sodium	445 mg

Ingredients

Cake:
1 (15.25 ounce) package carrot cake mix
1 cup water
2/3 cup vegetable oil
3 eggs
Filling:
2 1/2 cups milk
1 (5 ounce) package instant vanilla pudding

mix
1 (8 ounce) package cream cheese, softened
1 (8 ounce) container frozen whipped topping, thawed
Topping:
1 cup chopped almonds
1 cup shredded coconut
1 cup toffee baking bits

Directions

1. Coat a casserole dish nonstick spray then set your oven to 350 degrees before doing anything else.

2. Get a bowl, combine: eggs, cake mix, veggie oil, and water. With a mixer combine the mix into a batter. Then pour the mix into the casserole dish.

3. Cook the cake in the oven for 35 mins. Let the cake sit for 13 mins. Leave the oven on as the cake cools.

4. Get a 2nd bowl, combine: pudding mix and milk. Combine in the cream cheese and work everything until it is smooth.

5. Get a cookie sheet and layer your coconut and almond onto it then toast them in the oven for 7 mins. At this point the nuts should be aromatic.

6. Now begin to carefully slice your cake into cubes. Place one layer of cubes into a trifle dish then top the cake with the pudding mix about the same height as the layer cake then top the layer with some almonds, toffee, and coconut.

7. Continue layering in this manner until all the ingredients have been used up.

8. Enjoy.

Mariam's
October Cupcakes

🥣 Prep Time: 20 mins
🕐 Total Time: 35 mins

Servings per Recipe: 12	
Calories	374 kcal
Fat	17.7 g
Carbohydrates	51.2g
Protein	4 g
Cholesterol	72 mg
Sodium	322 mg

Ingredients

2 cups white sugar
1 cup butter, softened
2 eggs
1 teaspoon vanilla extract
2 cups all-purpose flour
1/4 cup finely chopped walnuts

1 teaspoon ground cinnamon
1 teaspoon baking powder
1/2 teaspoon baking soda
1/2 teaspoon salt
1/2 cup milk
1 cup finely grated carrots

Directions

1. Coat 12 sections of a muffin tin with nonstick spray or oil then set your oven to 300 degrees before doing anything else.
2. Get a bowl and place your butter and sugar in it. With a mixer work the butter until it is creamy then beat in your eggs one by one. Combine in the vanilla extract and beat the vanilla into the mix evenly.
3. Get a 2nd bowl, combine: salt, flour, baking soda, walnuts, baking powder, and cinnamon.
4. Add about one third of the dry mix to the butter mix then combine in the half of your milk and combine everything evenly.
5. Then add in the rest of the dry mix to the wet mix, stir everything, then add in the rest of the milk.
6. Once everything is combined nicely add in the carrots and work them into the batter.
7. Divide the batter between the muffin sections evenly then cook everything in the oven for 16 mins.
8. Enjoy.

ROASTED
Carrot Coins

Prep Time: 10 mins
Total Time: 22 mins

Servings per Recipe: 4
Calories	51 kcal
Fat	2.5 g
Carbohydrates	6.9g
Protein	0.7 g
Cholesterol	0 mg
Sodium	195 mg

Ingredients
4 carrots, washed, peeled into thin strips
2 teaspoons extra-virgin olive oil
1/4 teaspoon salt

Directions
1. Set your oven to 350 degrees before doing anything else.
2. Get a bowl for your carrots then add in your olive oil and stir everything to evenly coat the carrots. Add your salt and combine everything again to get the carrots coated once more.
3. Lay out your carrots evenly between two cookie sheets and position the racks in your oven in the following manner.
4. Place one oven rack in the highest position in oven and place another rack in the lowest position.
5. Now lay one sheet of sheets on the upmost rack and place the other sheet of carrots on the lowest rack.
6. Cook the carrots for about 7 mins then swap the racks and cook them for 7 more mins.
7. Enjoy.

Alternative
Carrot Gratin

🥣 Prep Time: 15 mins
🕐 Total Time: 1 hr 10 mins

Servings per Recipe: 8
Calories	304 kcal
Fat	20.5 g
Carbohydrates	20.9 g
Protein	10.4 g
Cholesterol	59 mg
Sodium	502 mg

Ingredients

12 carrots, peeled and sliced 1/4-inch thick
1/3 cup butter
1 onion, minced
3 cloves garlic, minced
1/4 cup all-purpose flour
salt to taste

2 cups milk
1 1/2 cups cubed Cheddar cheese, or to taste
1/4 teaspoon mustard powder
1/4 teaspoon white pepper
1/4 teaspoon celery seed
1/2 teaspoon salt
2 tablespoons butter, melted
1 cup soft bread crumbs

Directions

1. Coat a baking dish with oil then set your oven to 350 degrees before doing anything else.
2. Get your carrots boiling in salt water. Once the carrots are boiling set the heat to low, and let them cook for 5 mins. Remove all the liquid and place the carrots in a bowl.
3. Get a pot hot 1/3 cup of butter with a low level of heat, then begin to stir fry your garlic and onion in the butter for 7 mins. Add in some salt and stir everything. Then mix in your flour until evenly is smooth.
4. Continue to stir fry everything for about 7 more mins and everything is pasty.
5. Turn up a heat a bit to a medium level and slowly add in your milk and let the milk cook with the flour mix for 7 mins until it is thick.
6. Stir in your cheddar gradually waiting for the cheese to melt before adding in more. Continue adding cheese in this manner for about 12 mins until all the cheese has been melted and combined nicely into a sauce. Combine in: 1/2 tsp salt, mustard powder, celery seed, and white pepper and let the mix cook for 2 more mins. Then shut the heat.
7. Combine your carrots with this sauce then pour everything into the baking dish.
8. Get a small bowl and combine 2 tbsps of melted butter with the bread crumbs then garnish the carrots with the crumbly mix evenly.
9. For about 27 mins cook everything in the oven. Enjoy.

CARROT
Cake 101

Prep Time: 30 mins
Total Time: 2 hrs

Servings per Recipe: 15

Calories	616 kcal
Fat	30.2 g
Carbohydrates	83.5g
Protein	6.2 g
Cholesterol	70 mg
Sodium	540 mg

Ingredients

2 cups white sugar
3/4 cup vegetable oil
3 eggs
1 teaspoon vanilla extract
3/4 cup buttermilk
2 cups grated carrots
1 cup flaked coconut
1 (15 ounce) can crushed pineapple, drained
2 cups all-purpose flour

2 teaspoons baking soda
2 teaspoons ground cinnamon
1 1/2 teaspoons salt
1 cup chopped walnuts
1/2 cup butter
1 (8 ounce) package cream cheese
1 teaspoon vanilla extract
4 cups confectioners' sugar

Directions

1. Coat a casserole dish with nonstick spray then set your oven to 350 degrees before doing anything else.
2. Get a bowl, combine: buttermilk, sugar, vanilla, oil, and eggs. Whisk everything evenly then combine in the pineapple, carrots, vanilla, and coconut.
3. Get a 2nd bowl, sift: salt, flour, cinnamon, and baking soda.
4. Combine both bowl carefully and gradually and form an even batter. Combine in the nuts and stir everything.
5. Layer your batter into the casserole dish and cook the cake for 60 mins.
6. Get a 3d bowl, cream with a mixer: vanilla, margarine, confectioners, and cream cheese. Once the mix is smooth and creamy top your cake with it liberally and evenly when the cake is cool.
7. Enjoy.

Classical Northern
French Soufflé

Prep Time: 5 mins
Total Time: 1 hr 5 mins

Servings per Recipe: 6
Calories	309 kcal
Fat	17.6 g
Carbohydrates	34.8g
Protein	4.3 g
Cholesterol	93 mg
Sodium	508 mg

Ingredients

1 pound carrots, coarsely chopped
1/2 cup margarine
1 teaspoon vanilla extract
3 eggs

3 tablespoons all-purpose flour
1 teaspoon baking powder
1/2 teaspoon salt
3/4 cup white sugar

Directions

1. Coat a baking dish with oil then set your oven to 350 degrees before doing anything else.
2. Get a saucepan of water with salt boiling then once it is boiling add in your carrots. Let the carrots boil for 17 mins.
3. Now remove all the liquids and mash the carrots with a masher. Combine in the eggs, margarine, and vanilla extract. Combine everything evenly then sift the sugar, flour, salt, and baking powder into a separate bowl, then combine the dry mix with the carrots.
4. Combine the mix then place everything into the baking dish and cook the soufflé in the oven for about 45 mins.
5. Enjoy.

SWEETIE
Pie Carrots

Prep Time: 10 mins
Total Time: 40 mins

Servings per Recipe: 4
Calories	150 kcal
Fat	6 g
Carbohydrates	24.5g
Protein	1.2 g
Cholesterol	15 mg
Sodium	220 mg

Ingredients
1 pound carrots, cut into 2 inch pieces
2 tablespoons butter, diced
1/4 cup packed brown sugar
1 pinch salt
1 pinch ground black pepper

Directions
1. Get your carrots boiling in salt and water. Once the mix is boiling set the heat to low and let everything cook for about 20 - 25 mins.
2. Remove all the liquid and set the stove to very low heat. Place the carrots back into the pot and combine in the pepper, butter, salt, and brown sugar. Stir and cook for about 4 mins.
3. Enjoy.

Patricia's
Pot Luck Pudding

Prep Time: 20 mins
Total Time: 3 hrs

Servings per Recipe: 7

Calories	552 kcal
Fat	19.9 g
Carbohydrates	93.8g
Protein	3.6 g
Cholesterol	58 mg
Sodium	296 mg

Ingredients

1 cup grated carrots
1 cup peeled and shredded potatoes
1 cup white sugar
1 cup raisins
1 cup all-purpose flour
1 teaspoon baking soda
1 teaspoon ground cinnamon

1 teaspoon ground allspice
1 teaspoon ground cloves
1/2 cup butter
1/2 cup heavy whipping cream
1 cup white sugar
1 1/2 teaspoons vanilla extract

Directions

1. Get a bowl, combine: cloves, carrots, allspice, potatoes, cinnamon, sugar, baking soda, flour, and raisins.
2. Get a coffee can and put everything into the can. Place a covering of foil or wax paper on the can and place it in pot of boiling water.
3. Pour in about 4 inches of water to the pot and put a lid on the pot. Let everything boil gently for about 2 hours.
4. Once the cake is done get a saucepan and combine the following in it: vanilla, butter, sugar, and cream. Heat the mix until is wet and smooth then top your cake with the sweet glaze.
5. Enjoy.

HOW TO MAKE
a Carrot Pie

Prep Time: 30 mins
Total Time: 3 h 25 mins

Servings per Recipe: 8
Calories	232 kcal
Fat	9.2 g
Carbohydrates	33.7g
Protein	4 g
Cholesterol	48 mg
Sodium	167 mg

Ingredients

1 (9 inch) unbaked pie shell
3/4 cup sugar
2 cups chopped carrots
2 eggs

1 teaspoon ground cinnamon
1 teaspoon vanilla extract
3/4 cup milk

Directions

1. Set your oven to 400 degrees before doing anything else.
2. Get a pie dish and place your crust into it. Cook the pie crust in the oven for 4 mins then remove it.
3. Get your carrots boiling in a large pot of water for 12 mins, then remove all the liquid and begin to mash the carrots with a blender or by hand.
4. Get a bowl, combine: eggs, mashed carrots, and sugar. Whisk the mix nicely then combine in the vanilla and cinnamon. Slowly add in the milk and combine everything nicely. Pour the mix into the toasted pie crust.
5. Now cook the pie in the oven for 12 mins then set the heat to 350 and continue cooking the pie for 35 to 42 mins longer.
6. Enjoy.

Thanksgiving
Carrots

🥣 Prep Time: 10 mins
🕐 Total Time: 27 mins

Servings per Recipe: 6
Calories	195 kcal
Fat	7.9 g
Carbohydrates	32.9g
Protein	0.8 g
Cholesterol	21 mg
Sodium	149 mg

Ingredients

2 (8 ounce) packages carrots, peeled and cut into chunks
1 cup dried cranberries, or more to taste
1/4 cup chicken broth

1/4 cup butter, melted
1/4 cup dark brown sugar
1 pinch ground cinnamon, or to taste

Directions

1. Place your cranberries and carrots in a bowl.
2. Get a 2nd bowl, combine: brown sugar, butter, and chicken broth. Stir the mix evenly then top your carrots with the mixture.
3. Stir the mix then heat the carrots in the microwave with the highest level of heat for 5 mins. Stop the microwave stir the carrots carefully. Then continue to microwave them for 7 more mins.
4. Carefully remove the bowl from the microwave and let it sit for 7 mins then top the carrots with the cinnamon.
5. Enjoy.

CARROTS
from Florida

Prep Time: 15 mins
Total Time: 35 mins

Servings per Recipe: 4
Calories	228 kcal
Fat	17.4 g
Carbohydrates	18.8g
Protein	2 g
Cholesterol	33 mg
Sodium	344 mg

Ingredients
4 large carrots, halved
2 tablespoons honey
1 tablespoon frozen apple juice concentrate,
thawed
3 tablespoons minced fresh parsley
1/4 cup chopped toasted hazelnuts

1/4 teaspoon garlic powder
1/4 teaspoon ground nutmeg
1/2 teaspoon salt
1/4 teaspoon pepper
1/4 cup clarified butter

Directions
1. Place a steamer insert into a pot with about 2 inches of water. Get the water boiling then place your carrots into the pot. Place a lid on the pot and steam your carrots for 8 mins. Once the carrots are easy to handle use a grater to mince them down.
2. Get a bowl, combine: hazelnuts, carrots, parsley, honey, and apple juice concentrate.
3. Toss the mix then combine in the pepper, garlic powder, salt, and nutmeg. Toss everything again to distribute the spices evenly.
4. Get a frying pan hot with butter and then begin to fry your carrot mix in the hot butter until it warmed completely.
5. Enjoy.

Cream of
Carrot Casserole

Prep Time: 15 mins
Total Time: 45 mins

Servings per Recipe: 6
Calories	331 kcal
Fat	24.6 g
Carbohydrates	23.1g
Protein	6 g
Cholesterol	61 mg
Sodium	909 mg

Ingredients

5 cups sliced carrots
3 tablespoons butter
1 onion, chopped
1 (10.75 ounce) can condensed cream of celery soup

salt and pepper to taste
1/2 cup cubed processed cheese
2 cups seasoned croutons
1/3 cup melted butter

Directions

1. Coat a baking dish with oil then set your oven to 350 degrees before doing anything else.
2. Get your carrots boiling in water in a large pot for 9 mins. Remove the liquids then begin to stir fry your onions in another large pot, in butter. Once the onion are frying combine in the cheese, pepper, soup, and salt.
3. Stir everything again then combine in the carrots. Let the mix cook for 2 mins then place everything into the baking dish carefully.
4. Combine the carrot mix with one third a cup of melted butter and croutons. Evenly dispersed over the top of the carrot mix.
5. Cook everything in the oven for 25 mins.
6. Enjoy.

JUNE'S
Carrot Raisin Salad

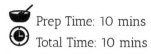 Prep Time: 10 mins

Total Time: 10 mins

Servings per Recipe: 6

Calories	393 kcal
Fat	30.3 g
Carbohydrates	29.8g
Protein	6.1 g
Cholesterol	0 mg
Sodium	81 mg

Ingredients

1 cup shredded carrots
1 cup finely chopped apple
1/2 cup raisins
1/2 cup golden raisins

1 cup whole almonds
1/2 cup vegetable oil
salt and ground black pepper to taste

Directions

1. Get a bowl, combine: almonds, carrots, apple, both raisins, and oil. Top everything with some pepper and salt and toss everything.

2. Enjoy.

October's
Creamy Carrot Soup

🥣 Prep Time: 15 mins
🕐 Total Time: 1 hr 30 mins

Servings per Recipe: 4
Calories	352 kcal
Fat	12.3 g
Carbohydrates	46.7g
Protein	15.1 g
Cholesterol	3 mg
Sodium	< 239 mg

Ingredients

3 tablespoons extra-virgin olive oil
1 onion, thinly sliced
1 clove garlic, minced
1 pound carrots, cut into thin half-rounds
1 tablespoon tomato paste

1/2 teaspoon ground chili pepper
1/4 teaspoon sea salt
3 cups water
1 cup lentils
salt and freshly ground black pepper to taste
1/4 cup Greek yogurt

Directions

1. Get your oil hot in a frying pan then begin to stir fry your onions for 7 mins. Combine in the garlic and continue frying everything for 3 more mins. Stir the mix then stir in your sea salt, carrots, chili pepper, and tomato paste. Stir the mix and let it fry for about 60 secs then shut the heat.
2. Get your water boiling in a large pot then combine in the lentils. Place a lid on the pot and set the heat to low. Let the lentils cook for 32 mins. Take off the lid and turn up the stove's heat to a medium level.
3. Combine in the onion mix and let everything simmer for about 3 more mins.
4. Add in some pepper and salt and let the lentil cool off for about 15 mins.
5. When eating your lentils and carrots top each dish with some yogurt liberally.
6. Enjoy.

CARROT
Dessert Squares

Prep Time: 30 mins
Total Time: 1 hr

Servings per Recipe: 30

Calories	289 kcal
Fat	18.7 g
Carbohydrates	28.8g
Protein	2.7 g
Cholesterol	41 mg
Sodium	218 mg

Ingredients

1 1/2 cups vegetable oil
2 cups white sugar
4 eggs, beaten
2 (4 ounce) jars carrot baby food
2 cups all-purpose flour
2 teaspoons baking soda
1 teaspoon salt

1 1/2 teaspoons ground cinnamon
1/2 cup chopped walnuts
1 (8 ounce) package cream cheese
1/4 pound butter, softened
2 cups confectioners' sugar
2 teaspoons vanilla extract

Directions

1. Coat two casserole dishes with flour and oil then set your oven to 350 degrees before doing anything else.
2. Get a bowl, combine: carrots, oil, eggs, and sugar.
3. Get a 2nd bowl, combine: cinnamon, flour, salt, baking soda.
4. Combine both bowls carefully and gradually. Then divide the mix between your casserole dishes.
5. Cook everything in the oven for about 28 to 32 mins. Then let the dish cool.
6. As the dish is cooling get a bowl, and whisk with a mixer: vanilla, butter, powdered sugar, and cream cheese. Once the mix is nice and smooth top the contents of your casserole dishes with the frosting evenly.
7. Gently cut your carrot cakes into dessert bars.
8. Enjoy.

Rustic Roasted
Carrots & Yams

Prep Time: 20 mins
Total Time: 1 hr 20 mins

Servings per Recipe: 12
Calories   362 kcal
Fat   5 g
Carbohydrates   74.1g
Protein   7.4 g
Cholesterol   0 mg
Sodium   161 mg

Ingredients

7 large potatoes, peeled and quartered
9 carrots, julienned
4 large sweet potatoes, peeled and quartered

2 onions, quartered
salt and pepper to taste
1/4 cup vegetable oil

Directions

1. Set you oven to 350 degrees before doing anything else.
2. Get a casserole dish and add in 1/3 a cup of water into it.
3. Begin to layer the following in your casserole dish: onions, potatoes, yams, and carrots. Top the layers with some pepper and salt liberally.
4. Top everything with the oil.
5. Place a covering of foil on the dish and roast everything in the oven for about 2 hours.
6. Enjoy.

MEDITERRANEAN
Carrots

Prep Time: 15 mins
Total Time: 30 mins

Servings per Recipe: 2
Calories	197 kcal
Fat	17.4 g
Carbohydrates	10.3g
Protein	2.4 g
Cholesterol	54 mg
Sodium	78 mg

Ingredients
1 teaspoon olive oil
3 carrots, shredded
1 fennel bulb, trimmed and diced
1/2 teaspoon ground coriander
1/4 teaspoon fennel seeds
1/3 cup heavy cream

Directions
1. Fry your fennel and carrots in olive oil in a frying pan for a few mins then add in your fennel seeds and coriander. Stir everything then continue to fry it for another min. Combine in the heavy cream then set the heat to its lowest level.
2. Let the mix gently boil for about 4 to 6 mins until all the cream has been soaked up by the veggies.
3. Enjoy.

Indian Style
Spicy Raisins Carrots

🥣 Prep Time: 10 mins
🕐 Total Time: 55 mins

Servings per Recipe: 6
Calories	227 kcal
Fat	11 g
Carbohydrates	30.6g
Protein	1.8 g
Cholesterol	0 mg
Sodium	206 mg

Ingredients
1 1/2 pounds carrots, sliced
1/3 cup vegetable wine or more to taste
6 tablespoons margarine
1/2 teaspoon ground nutmeg

1/2 teaspoon ground cinnamon
1/4 teaspoon ground ginger
2/3 cup raisins
2 tablespoons light brown sugar

Directions
1. Add the following to a large pot: ginger, carrots, cinnamon, broth, nutmeg, and margarine. Stir the mix then get everything boiling.
2. Set the heat to low and let the mix gently boil for about 28 to 32 mins.
3. Combine in the brown sugar and raisins into the carrots and get everything simmer again until everything coated with sugar sauce.
4. Enjoy.

DEEP
Fried Carrots

Prep Time: 15 mins
Total Time: 30 mins

Servings per Recipe: 4
Calories	592 kcal
Fat	47.1 g
Carbohydrates	36.5g
Protein	8.3 g
Cholesterol	93 mg
Sodium	647 mg

Ingredients
4 carrots, julienned
1 onion, cut into 1/4-inch slices
1 bunch green onions, chopped
1 cup all-purpose flour

1 teaspoon salt
1/4 teaspoon ground black pepper
2 eggs
2 quarts oil for deep frying

Directions
1. Get a bowl, whisk: eggs, carrots, pepper, onion, salt, flour, and green onions. Whisk the mix evenly.
2. As you are preparing your carrots your oil should be heating in a Dutch oven. Once the oil has reached a frying temperature fry dollops of the mix in the oil for about 2 to 3 mins each side. Frying time depends on the heat of your oil.
3. Enjoy.

Circular
Carrot Cake

Prep Time: 20 mins
Total Time: 1 hr

Servings per Recipe: 8

Calories	204 kcal
Fat	7.3 g
Carbohydrates	31.3g
Protein	3.9 g
Cholesterol	62 mg
Sodium	351 mg

Ingredients

1/4 cup butter
1/2 cup brown sugar
2 eggs
1 teaspoon lemon juice

1 1/4 cups all-purpose flour
1 teaspoon baking powder
1/2 teaspoon baking soda
1/2 teaspoon salt
2 cups grated carrots

Directions

1. Coat a ring mold with oil then set your oven 350 degrees before doing anything else.
2. Get a bowl, combine: brown sugar, and butter. Whisk the mix until it is creamy then combine in the lemon juice and eggs one by one.
3. Slowly sift in the salt, baking soda, baking powder, and flour. Once the mix is combined evenly combine in the carrots.
4. Place the mix into the greased mold and cook everything in the oven for 40 mins.
5. Enjoy..

DILL &
Garlic Rainy Day Soup

Prep Time: 20 mins
Total Time: 1 h 40 mins

Servings per Recipe: 6
Calories	234 kcal
Fat	15.9 g
Carbohydrates	22.8g
Protein	2.6 g
Cholesterol	41 mg
Sodium	849 mg

Ingredients
3 pounds carrots, chopped
6 cups chicken stock
3 cloves garlic, chopped

2 tablespoons dried dill weed
1/4 pound butter
1 1/2 teaspoons salt

Directions
1. Get the following boiling in a larger pot: butter, chicken stock, salt, carrots, dill weed, and garlic. Once everything is boiling set the heat to low and let the mix gently cook for 35 mins.
2. With an immersion blender, or working in batches with a conventional blender, puree everything in the pot. And continue to gently cook the soup for another 35 mins.
3. Add in some extra garlic and dill.
4. Enjoy.

Grand
Ole Carrots

Prep Time: 15 mins
Total Time: 30 min

Servings per Recipe: 12

Calories	145 kcal
Fat	9.3 g
Carbohydrates	15.4g
Protein	0.7 g
Cholesterol	0 mg
Sodium	44 mg

Ingredients

2 pounds carrots, sliced
1 small onion, thinly sliced
1 small green bell pepper, cut into thin strips
1/2 cup vegetable oil

1/2 cup white sugar
1/4 cup distilled white vinegar
2 teaspoons almond extract
1 teaspoon dried basil

Directions

1. Get your carrots boiling in water in a big pot with a lid on the pot until the carrots somewhat soft but still firm.
2. Transfer the carrots along with the pepper and onion into a bowl.
3. In a 2nd pot begin to stir and heat the: basil, oil, almond extract, vinegar, and sugar. Stir and heat the mix until the sugar is completely dissolved with medium level of heat.
4. Combine the basil mix with the carrots. Place a covering of plastic on the bowl and put everything in the fridge for 7 hours.
5. Enjoy..

CARROT
Patties

Prep Time: 15 mins

Total Time: 40 mins

Servings per Recipe: 12

Calories	206 kcal
Fat	11.5 g
Carbohydrates	22.5g
Protein	4.1 g
Cholesterol	34 mg
Sodium	300 mg

Ingredients
2 cups shredded carrots
2 eggs
1/2 cup mayonnaise
1 medium onion, minced
2 tablespoons olive oil

1 clove garlic, chopped
salt and pepper to taste
6 cups soft bread crumbs
4 cups whole wheat flake cereal, crumbled

Directions
1. Set your oven to 375 degrees before doing anything else.
2. Get a bowl for your carrots and cook them in the microwave with high heat for 2.5 mins.
3. Get a 2nd bigger bowl, combine: carrots, eggs, pepper, mayo, salt, onion, garlic, and olive oil. Combine everything evenly then combine in the bread crumbs.
4. Form the crumbly mix into 12 burgers then coat the burgers with the cereal. Place the cereal in a bowl to make it easier to dredge the carrots in it.
5. Get a casserole dish and coat with some non-stick spray or oil then cook the burgers in the oven for 27 mins.
6. Flip the patties at the half way make.
7. Enjoy.

Creamy
Carrot Snack

Prep Time: 30 mins
Total Time: 1 hr

Servings per Recipe: 7
Calories	198 kcal
Fat	6.4 g
Carbohydrates	36.2g
Protein	1.3 g
Cholesterol	8 mg
Sodium	241 mg

Ingredients

3 cups julienned carrots
1 (20 ounce) can pineapple tidbits, drained
1/2 cup raisins

1/2 cup diced celery (optional)
2/3 cup creamy salad dressing
2 teaspoons white sugar

Directions

1. Get a salad bowl, combine: celery, carrots, raisins, and pineapple.
2. Get a 2nd bowl, combine: sugar and dressing. Toss the carrot mix with the dressing mix and place a covering of plastic on the bowl.
3. Put everything in the fridge overnight.
4. Enjoy.

2-INGREDIENT
Caribbean Carrots

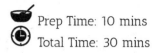 Prep Time: 10 mins
Total Time: 30 mins

Servings per Recipe: 8
Calories	52 kcal
Fat	0.8 g
Carbohydrates	11.2g
Protein	0.9 g
Cholesterol	0 mg
Sodium	67 mg

Ingredients
2 pounds carrots, chopped
1 (10 ounce) can cream of coconut

Directions
1. Get the following simmering in a pot: cream coconut and carrots. Once the mix is simmering let it gently cook for 18 to 22 mins.
2. Enjoy.

Pickled
Carrots

Prep Time: 15 mins
Total Time: 30 mins

Servings per Recipe: 16
Calories	106 kcal
Fat	3.9 g
Carbohydrates	18.1g
Protein	1 g
Cholesterol	0 mg
Sodium	145 mg

Ingredients

2 pounds carrots, sliced
1 green bell pepper, seeded and diced
1 small onion, diced

1/2 cup white vinegar
1/4 cup vegetable oil
1 (10.75 ounce) can condensed tomato soup
3/4 cup sugar

Directions

1. Get a pot for your carrots and get them boiling in water and salt. Let the boil for 7 mins. Remove the liquid and put the carrots in a bowl.
2. At the same time heat and stir the following in a 2nd pot: sugar, vinegar, tomato soup, and oil. Get this mix boiling and let it cook for 2 mins then shut the heat.
3. Combine your onion and bell peppers with the carrots and toss everything. Combine in the tomato mix and toss everything again.
4. Enjoy.

SUNDAY'S SIDE
of Long Grain Rice

Prep Time: 15 mins
Total Time: 55 mins

Servings per Recipe: 12
Calories	285 kcal
Fat	14.1 g
Carbohydrates	36.3g
Protein	3.3 g
Cholesterol	38 mg
Sodium	514 mg

Ingredients
1 cup sliced carrots
3 tablespoons minced onion
4 1/2 cups water
2 teaspoons salt
2 cups uncooked long grain white rice

1/2 cup white sugar
1 cup half-and-half cream
3/4 cup butter

Directions
1. Get the following boiling in a pot: salt, carrots, water, and onions. Once the mix ix boiling stir everything, set the heat to low, and let the dish cook for 12 mins. Combine in the rice, set the heat lower and place a lid on the pot.
2. Let the rice gently cook for 22 mind.
3. Now combine in the butter, half and half, and sugar with the rice and fluff everything.
4. Shut the heat.
5. Enjoy.

Mashed
Carrots

Prep Time: 20 mins
Total Time: 1 h 20 mins

Servings per Recipe: 8
Calories	235 kcal
Fat	13.1 g
Carbohydrates	20.6g
Protein	9.8 g
Cholesterol	37 mg
Sodium	351 mg

Ingredients

2 pounds carrots, cut into 2 inch pieces
2 tablespoons butter
1 onion, minced
8 ounces sharp Cheddar cheese, shredded

1 green bell pepper, minced
1/4 cup fresh parsley, chopped
salt and pepper to taste
3/4 cup dry bread crumbs

Directions

1. Get your carrots boiling in water until they are soft.
2. Now coat a baking dish with oil then set your oven to 350 degrees before doing anything else.
3. Once the carrots are soft place them in a bowl and mash them with a masher. Combine in your pepper, butter, salt, onion, parsley, cheese, and green pepper.
4. Layer everything into your casserole dish and top it with some bread crumbs evenly. Cook everything for about 38 to 42 mins in the oven.
5. Enjoy.

CHIVE
and Carrot
Spread

Prep Time: 15 mins
Total Time: 35 mins

Servings per Recipe: 4
Calories	164 kcal
Fat	17.4 g
Carbohydrates	2.7g
Protein	< 0.5 g
Cholesterol	46 mg
Sodium	220 mg

Ingredients
8 parsnips, peeled and cut into 2 inch pieces
2 carrots, peeled and cut into 2-inch pieces
1/4 cup snipped chives

6 tablespoons butter, divided
sea salt and freshly ground black pepper to taste

Directions
1. Get your carrots and parsnips boiling in water with salt. Once the mix is boiling, set the heat to low, place a lid on the pot and let the carrots cook for 17 mins.
2. Remove all the liquid and then place everything back into the pot. Set the heat to its lowest level then combine in 3 tbsps of butter and your chives. Stir everything together then with an immersion blender puree the carrots and parsnips.
3. Combine in another 3 tbsps of butter and keep processing the mix with the immersion blender until it smooth.
4. Top with some pepper and salt.
5. Enjoy.

Carmen's
Tangy Carrots

🥣 Prep Time: 20 mins
🕐 Total Time: 35 mins

Servings per Recipe: 6
Calories   224 kcal
Fat   16.9 g
Carbohydrates   16.9g
Protein   2.5 g
Cholesterol   11 mg
Sodium   245 mg

Ingredients

8 carrots, julienned
1 teaspoon butter
2 tablespoons grated onion
1/2 cup mayonnaise

2 tablespoons creamy-style horseradish sauce
1/4 teaspoon pepper
1/2 cup bread crumbs
1/2 teaspoon paprika

Directions

1. Add about 1 of water to a larger pot then add in your carrots and get everything boiling. Let the carrots cook for 6 mins them remove the liquid.
2. Now coat a baking dish with some butter and then set your oven to 375 degrees before doing anything else.
3. Lay your carrots in the greased dish then get a bowl, combine: bread crumbs, onion, paprika, mayo, pepper, and horseradish.
4. Top your carrots with the crumbly mix then cook everything in the oven for 16 mins.
5. Enjoy.

VEGETARIAN
Carrot Burgers

Prep Time: 10 mins
Total Time: 1 hr

Servings per Recipe: 4
Calories	236 kcal
Fat	12.6 g
Carbohydrates	22.5g
Protein	9.1 g
Cholesterol	186 mg
Sodium	489 mg

Ingredients
1 pound carrots, grated
1 clove garlic, minced
4 eggs
1/4 cup all-purpose flour

1/4 cup bread crumbs or matzo meal
1/2 teaspoon salt
1 pinch ground black pepper
2 tablespoons vegetable oil

Directions
1. Combine the following in a big bowl: black pepper, carrots, salt, garlic, bread crumbs, flour, and eggs.
2. Get your oil hot in a skillet then shape the crumbly mix into burgers. Fry each burger until it is crispy on both sides.
3. Enjoy.

Canadian Style
Brown Sugar Carrots

🥣 Prep Time: 15 mins
🕐 Total Time: 35 mins

Servings per Recipe: 4
Calories	117 kcal
Fat	6 g
Carbohydrates	16.1g
Protein	1 g
Cholesterol	15 mg
Sodium	401 mg

Ingredients

3 cups peeled and sliced carrots
2 tablespoons butter
2 tablespoons brown sugar

1 1/2 tablespoons chopped fresh dill
1/2 teaspoon salt
1/2 teaspoon black pepper

Directions

1. Get a frying pan and put your carrots in it. Then cover them in water and get everything boiling. Once the mix is boiling let everything cook until all the water is gone. At this point the carrots should be soft then combine in the pepper, butter, salt, dill, and brown sugar.
2. Stir the mix so all the carrots are evenly coated.
3. Enjoy.

HONEY BUTTER
Bae Carrots

Prep Time: 5 mins
Total Time: 25 mins

Servings per Recipe: 4

Calories	402 kcal
Fat	23.3 g
Carbohydrates	50.7g
Protein	1.4 g
Cholesterol	61 mg
Sodium	249 mg

Ingredients
1 (16 ounce) package baby carrots
1/2 cup butter
3 tablespoons honey
1/2 cup brown sugar

Directions
1. Get your carrots boiling in a saucepan covered with salted water. Let the carrots cook for 17 mins. After the time has elapsed empty the water and let the carrots sit in the pot covered for about 4 mins with no heat.
2. Set the heat to low now and add in the butter. Let the butter melt then combine in the brown sugar and the honey. Continue to stir and heat the mix for 4 more mins.
3. Enjoy.

A Stew
in Dublin

🥣 Prep Time: 30 mins
🕐 Total Time: 50 mins

Servings per Recipe: 6
Calories	161 kcal
Fat	3.1 g
Carbohydrates	31.3g
Protein	3.8 g
Cholesterol	< 1 mg
Sodium	< 1196 mg

Ingredients

4 large carrots, thinly sliced
2 large potatoes, thinly sliced
1 large onion, thinly sliced
1/4 medium head green cabbage, thinly sliced
2 cloves garlic, smashed

6 cups chicken stock
1 tablespoon olive oil
1/4 teaspoon dried thyme
1/4 teaspoon dried basil
1 teaspoon dried parsley
1 teaspoon salt
ground black pepper to taste

Directions

1. Get the following boiling in a larger pot like a Dutch oven: pepper, carrots, salt, potatoes, parsley, onion, basil, cabbage, thyme, garlic, olive oil, and chicken stock.
2. Once the mix is boiling set the heat to low and let everything gently cook for 22 mins. With an immersion blender puree everything to form a soup.
3. If you do not have an immersion blender you can puree the solids in batches with a conventional blender placing the puree into a 2nd pot until everything has been processed and combining the puree with the original liquid.
4. Enjoy.

NORTH AFRICAN
Carrot Sesame Apricot Spread

Prep Time: 10 mins
Total Time: 22 mins

Servings per Recipe: 10	
Calories	65 kcal
Fat	2.1 g
Carbohydrates	12.1g
Protein	0.6 g
Cholesterol	0 mg
Sodium	210 mg

Ingredients
1 pound carrots, peeled and thinly sliced
3 cloves garlic, thinly sliced
1 (2 inch) piece fresh ginger root, peeled and thinly sliced
3/4 teaspoon salt, divided
1/3 cup apricot preserves

2 tablespoons fresh lemon juice
4 teaspoons toasted sesame oil
1 1/2 teaspoons ground coriander
1/8 teaspoon cayenne pepper

Directions
1. Pour 2 cups of water in a larger pot then combine in you're: 1/4 tsp salt, carrots, ginger, and garlic. Get everything boiling then once it is set the heat to low, place a lid on the pot, and let the mix cook for 11 mins.
2. Remove the liquids then add the mix to a blender. Also add in the cayenne, 1/2 tsp salt, coriander, apricot, sesame oil, and lemon juice.
3. Puree the mix into a dip.
4. Enjoy.

4-Ingredient
Carrots

Prep Time: 10 mins
Total Time: 1 hr

Servings per Recipe: 4
Calories	98 kcal
Fat	5.1 g
Carbohydrates	11.2g
Protein	3 g
Cholesterol	4 mg
Sodium	381 mg

Ingredients

1 pound carrots, peeled
1 tablespoon olive oil
1/2 teaspoon garlic salt
1/4 cup grated Parmesan cheese, or more
to taste

Directions

1. Cover a casserole dish with foil then set your oven to 375 degrees before doing anything else.
2. Get a bowl, combine: garlic salt and olive oil. Combine in your carrots and toss them evenly in the mix. Layer your carrots into the casserole dish and cook them in the oven for 40 mins. Top the carrots with the parmesan evenly and continue to cook everything for about 7 more mins.
3. Add some parmesan before serving.
4. Enjoy.

BACKROAD
Canning Carrots

Prep Time: 15 mins
Total Time: 35 mins

Servings per Recipe: 4
Calories	74 kcal
Fat	0.1 g
Carbohydrates	< 18.3g
Protein	0.9 g
Cholesterol	0 mg
Sodium	28 mg

Ingredients
1/2 cup distilled white vinegar
1/4 cup white sugar
1 small carrot, peeled and cut into matchsticks

1 daikon radish, peeled and cut into matchsticks
2 tablespoons chopped fresh cilantro
1 Thai chili pepper, seeded and chopped

Directions
1. Gat your sugar and vinegar heating in a pot until the sugar is evenly combined.
2. Shut the heat and place the liquid in the fridge until it is cold.
3. Get a jar and put your carrot and radish in the jar. Also place in the jar your chili pepper and cilantro. Add the vinegar into the jar and place the lid on them tightly.
4. Place everything in the fridge overnight.
5. Enjoy.

Hong Kong
Carrot Vegetarian Dump Dinner

🥣 Prep Time: 10 mins
🕐 Total Time: 8 hr 40 min

Servings per Recipe: 6
Calories   140 kcal
Fat   2.7 g
Carbohydrates   27.5g
Protein   3.3 g
Cholesterol   0 mg
Sodium   770 mg

Ingredients

2 pounds baby carrots
1/2 cup orange juice concentrate
1/4 cup tamari sauce
2 cloves garlic, minced

1 teaspoon minced fresh ginger
1 teaspoon grated orange zest
1 tablespoon Asian (toasted) sesame oil
1 tablespoon honey

Directions

1. Simply all the ingredients to the crock pot of slow cooker and stir. Place the lid on the cooker and let the mix cook for 8 hours on low high then for 40 mins with High heat.
2. Enjoy.

PEANUT
Honey Carrots

Prep Time: 10 mins
Total Time: 50 mins

Servings per Recipe: 4
Calories	204 kcal
Fat	10.4 g
Carbohydrates	29.1g
Protein	1.2 g
Cholesterol	0 mg
Sodium	85 mg

Ingredients
8 carrots, peeled
3 tablespoons peanut oil
1/4 cup honey
salt and ground black pepper to taste

Directions
1. Set your oven to 350 degrees before doing anything else.
2. Get a casserole dish for your carrots and coat them evenly with the peanut oil. Toss everything then top the veggies with the honey and toss them again. Add your pepper and salt and toss one more time.
3. Cook the carrots in the oven for 50 mins.
4. Enjoy.

Lunch Box
Almond and Cranberry Salad

Prep Time: 20 mins
Total Time: 1 hr 30 min

Servings per Recipe: 6
Calories	295 kcal
Fat	19.7 g
Carbohydrates	23.8g
Protein	7.6 g
Cholesterol	14 mg
Sodium	370 mg

Ingredients
2 pounds carrots, peeled and thinly sliced on the diagonal
1/2 cup slivered almonds
2 cloves garlic, minced
1/4 cup extra-virgin olive oil
salt and ground black pepper to taste
1 teaspoon honey
1 tablespoon cider vinegar
1/3 cup dried cranberries
1 (4 ounce) package crumbled Danish blue cheese
2 cups arugula

Directions
1. Set your oven to 400 degrees before doing anything else.
2. Get a bowl, combine: garlic, carrots, and almonds. Top everything with the olive oil then with pepper and salt.
3. Lay the carrots into a casserole dish. Then cook them in the oven for 35 mins. Let the carrots lose their heat then place them in a bowl. Top the carrots with your vinegar and honey and combine everything nicely.
4. Combine in the blue cheese and cranberries and combine the salad again. Add in the arugula and divide the salad into servings or place the mix in the fridge covered until you are ready to eat.
5. Enjoy.

PLUMS, TOMATOES, and Samosas (Indian Style)

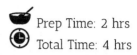 Prep Time: 2 hrs
Total Time: 4 hrs

Servings per Recipe: 15
Calories   163.5 g
Cholesterol   1.2mg
Sodium   230.6mg
Carbohydrates   27.5g
Protein   3.1

Ingredients

2 tbsps pine nuts
2 C. coarsely chopped plums
2 tbsps shallots, chopped
1 1/2 tsps olive oil
1 1/2 tsps butter
2 medium tomatoes, quartered
1 garlic clove, chopped
1 tbsp sugar
1/2 tsp harissa, see appendix
1 thyme, sprig
1 vanilla bean
1/2 tsp chopped fresh basil
1/4 tsp salt
cooking spray
1/2 C. thinly sliced yellow onion
1 lb Yukon gold potato, peeled and cut into
1/4-inch cubes

1/2 C. carrot, chopped
2 1/2 tsps red curry paste
1 garlic clove, diced
1 C. water
1/3 C. light coconut milk
2 tsps fresh lime juice
1/4 tsp salt
1 tsp ground turmeric
1/2 tsp ground ginger
1/2 tsp ground cinnamon
6 3/4 oz. all-purpose flour
1/2 tsp salt
1/4 tsp baking soda
1/4 C. hot water
6 tbsps fresh lemon juice
7 tsps peanut oil, divided

Directions

1. Begin by toasting your pine nuts for 3 mins with no oil in a large pot, then add in the garlic, plums, tomatoes, shallots, butter, and olive oil.

2. Get the mixing gently boiling, then set the heat to low, and continue to simmer the mix for 35 mins. Stir the mix every 5 mins.

3. Now combine in: the vanilla bean, sugar, thyme, and harissa.

4. Stir the mix and continue cooking everything for 25 more mins.

5. Now shut the heat, place a lid on the pot, and let the contents sit for 40 mins.

6. Take out the vanilla and thyme and throw them away. Then add in 1/4 tsp of salt and the basil. Stir the mix.

7. Get a frying pan hot with nonstick spray then begin to fry your potatoes and onions for 7 mins, set the heat to low, and stir in the garlic, curry paste, and carrots.

8. Continue to cook the carrots for 7 mins while mixing everything.
9. Combine in the coconut milk and 1 C. of water and get the mix boiling.
10. Once the mix is boiling set the heat to low, and continue to simmer everything for 17 mins until most of the moisture has cooked out.
11. Now combine in 1/4 tsp of salt and the lime juice.
12. Stir the mix then place everything into a bowl.
13. Let the potatoes lose their heat then mash everything together.
14. Get a separate frying pan and begin to toast your cinnamon, turmeric and ginger in it for 1 min then remove the spices to the side.
15. Now add the following to the bowl of a food processor: baking soda, flour, 1/2 tsp salt, and toasted cinnamon mix.
16. Process the mix a bit to evenly combine it then add in the following: 1 tbsp peanut oil, 1/4 C. hot water, and lemon juice.
17. Process the mix again until you have a dough.
18. Get a bowl and coat it with nonstick spray and place the dough in the bowl.
19. Place a damp kitchen towel over the bowl and let it sit for 20 mins.
20. Now break your dough into twelve pieces and flatten each into a circle.
21. In the middle of each circle add 2 tbsps of the potato mix. Coat the outside of each piece of dough with some water and shape everything into a semi-circle and seal each, with a fork.
22. Do this for all your dough and potato mix.
23. Now begin to fry half of the samosas in 2 tsp of hot peanut oil for 5 mins.
24. Flip each one and continue frying them for 4 more mins.
25. Now fry the rest of the samosas in an additional 2 tsp of oil for the same amount of time.
26. Top the samosas, with the harissa mix, when serving them.
27. Enjoy.

KALE
& Sweet Potato Stew

Prep Time: 40 mins
Total Time: 1 h 25 mins

Servings per Recipe: 8
Calories   249 kcal
Fat   15.4 mg
Carbohydrates   18.8 g
Protein   10.4 g
Cholesterol   30 mg
Sodium   1866 mg

Ingredients
1 large onion, diced
2 tbsps olive oil
8 oz. Spanish beef sausage, cut into 1/2 inch pieces
3 stalks celery, diced
3 carrots, diced
2 tsps ground cumin
1 tbsp paprika
1/2 tsp ground turmeric
2 tsps kosher salt
1 tsp freshly ground black pepper

1 pinch saffron threads
5 garlic cloves, diced
2 sweet potatoes, peeled and cut into 1-inch pieces
8 C. chicken broth
4 C. lacinato kale, washed, stemmed, and torn into pieces
1 lemon, juiced
salt and pepper to taste
1 pinch harissa, or to taste, see appendix
1 tbsp chopped fresh flat-leaf parsley

Directions
1. Stir fry your onions in olive oil, in a large pot, for 10 mins then combine in the chorizo and fry the sausage for 5 more mins.
2. Stir in the carrots and celery.
3. Continue frying the veggies for 5 mins then combine in: the garlic, cumin, saffron, turmeric, kosher salt, paprika, and black pepper.
4. Combine in the spices then continue frying everything for 4 more mins then combine in the broth and sweet potatoes.
5. Stir the mix again and get everything boiling.
6. Once the mix is boiling, set the heat to low, and simmer the mix for 25 mins.
7. Combine in the kale and cook the stew for 12 more mins then add some more pepper, salt, and the lemon juice.
8. When serving the stew top it with some parsley and harissa.
9. Enjoy.

Spicy
Carrot Paste

Prep Time: 5 mins
Total Time: 15 min

Servings per Recipe: 1
Calories   381.4
Cholesterol   0.0mg
Sodium   100.5mg
Carbohydrates   14.7g
Protein   1.5g

Ingredients

4 large carrots, peeled and roughly
chopped
2 garlic cloves, peeled and chopped
1/3 C. olive oil

1 tsp harissa, see appendix
sea salt
fresh ground pepper

Directions

1. Get your carrots boiling in water.
2. Once the carrots are soft remove all the liquids and place them into the bowl of a food processor and add in the garlic.
3. Begin to the puree the carrots and garlic then add the oil in a slow stream and continue pureeing the mix.
4. Now combine in the harissa and continue to puree everything until you have a smooth paste then add in some pepper and salt.
5. Stir the mix for a few secs and serve.
6. Enjoy.

VEGAN ZUCCHINI
(Tunisian Style)

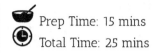

Prep Time: 15 mins
Total Time: 25 mins

Servings per Recipe: 3
Calories   111.8
Cholesterol   0.0mg
Sodium   34.8mg
Carbohydrates   6.7g
Protein   1.4

Ingredients

1/2 lb zucchini
2 carrots
2 tbsps olive oil
1 garlic clove, diced
1/2 tbsp harissa, see appendix
1/4 tsp ground cumin
1/4 tsp caraway seed

juice of half lemon
plain yogurt
fresh cilantro
salt, to taste
black pepper, to taste

Directions

1. Get a bowl, combine: olive oil, garlic clove, harissa, cumin, caraway, and lemon juice.
2. Get a casserole dish and place your carrots and zucchini in it. Top them with the olive oil mix evenly then place a covering of plastic on the dish and let the veggie sit for 60 mins.
3. Now get a grill hot and coat the grate with oil.
4. Grill the veggies for about 10 mins or until you find that the outside is slightly charred but the inside is tender.
5. Place the veggies in a dish for serving then top them with some pepper and salt.
6. Now add your cilantro evenly over everything and serve the dish with some yogurt.
7. Enjoy.

Spicy
Garbanzo Dip

🥣 Prep Time: 30 mins
🕐 Total Time: 3 hrs

Servings per Recipe: 4
Calories   840.8
Cholesterol   0.0mg
Sodium   58.1mg
Carbohydrates   108.1g
Protein   30.3

Ingredients
2 C. dried garbanzo beans
1 carrot, peeled and cut in half
1 medium Spanish onion, cut in half
4 garlic cloves, peeled
2 eggplants, cut in half lengthwise

1/4 C. olive oil
2 birds eye chilies, cut in half, seeds removed
2 tbsps olive oil
1 tsp harissa, see appendix
1 tsp ground cumin

Directions
1. Let your chickpeas sit submerged in water overnight. Then remove all the liquids.
2. Get the following boiling in water, in a large pot: 4 C. of water, chickpeas, onions, and carrots.
3. Once the mix is boiling, set the heat to low, and let the contents cook for 90 mins.
4. Set your oven to 300 degrees before doing anything else.
5. Now place one C. of the liquid to the side and remove the rest.
6. Get a bowl, combine: 1/4 C. of olive oil, eggplant, and garlic.
7. Stir the mix to evenly coat everything then place the mix into a casserole dish.
8. Cook the eggplants in the oven for 50 mins then add the chilies to the dish and keep cooking the mix for 12 more mins.
9. Remove the insides of your eggplant and place them into the bowl of a food processor.
10. Combine in the 3 tsp of the reserved liquid, garlic and chilies, 2 tbsp olive oil, cumin, harissa, and chickpeas.
11. Process the mix into a smooth paste and add in some more of the reserved liquid if needed. The mix should be creamy.
12. Serve the mix with some toasted pita rounds.
13. Enjoy.

PISTACHIO and Fig Tagine

🍳 Prep Time: 25 mins
⏰ Total Time: 3 h 40 mins

Servings per Recipe: 4
Calories 767.0
Cholesterol 161.0mg
Sodium 573.4mg
Carbohydrates 37.0g
Protein 41.6g

Ingredients

2 tbsps olive oil
2 tsps ground coriander
2 tsps ground cumin
1 1/2 tsps ground cinnamon
1 1/2 tsps turmeric
1 tsp grated lemon, zest of
1 1/2 tbsps lemon juice
1 1/2 tsps harissa, see appendix
8 chicken thighs, skin removed
2 tbsps olive oil
2 onions, chopped
2 carrots, sliced into coins

2 cloves garlic, diced
2 tsps grated ginger
6 oz. button mushrooms, halved
8 large dried figs, coarsely chopped
2 tbsps all-purpose flour
1 3/4 C. chicken stock
2 tbsps tomato paste
1 tbsp lemon juice
3/4 C. pitted black olives
1/3 C. shelled pistachios
2 tbsps chopped fresh parsley

Directions

1. Get a bowl, combine: harissa, 2 tbsps olive oil, lemon juice, coriander, lemon zest, cumin, turmeric, and cinnamon.

2. Stir the mix until it is smooth then cover your pieces of chicken with it.

3. Sear the chicken all over then place the meat in the crock of a slow cooker.

4. Begin to fry your garlic, carrots, and onions for 7 mins then add in the flour, figs, and mushrooms.

5. Stir the mix and continue to cook everything for 2 more mins.

6. Now combine in the lemon juice, tomato paste, and chicken stock.

7. Stir the mix again and get everything boiling.

8. Once the mix is boiling pour everything in the slow cooker.

9. Place a lid on the crock pot and cook everything for 4 hrs with a high level of heat.

10. When 30 mins of cooking time is left, add in your pistachios, parsley, and olives to the slow cooker and let everything finish simmering.

11. Enjoy.

North African
Breakfast

Prep Time: 15 mins
Total Time: 45 mins

Servings per Recipe: 6
Calories   178.2
Cholesterol   310.0mg
Sodium   366.3mg
Carbohydrates   9.3g
Protein   11.6

Ingredients
1 lb carrot, sliced
1 tbsp caraway seed, freshly ground
1 tbsp harissa, see appendix
4 large garlic cloves, diced
1/2 tsp salt

pepper, freshly ground
8 large eggs, fresh
2 eggs, hard cooked and finely chopped
1/4 C. fresh flat-leaf parsley, chopped
1 tbsp extra virgin olive oil

Directions
1. Get your oven's broiler hot and begin to steam your carrots over 2 inches of boiling water, with a steamer insert, for 25 mins, with a lid on the pot.
2. Add the carrots to the bowl of a food processor and begin to puree them, combine in some pepper, some salt, caraway, garlic, and the harissa.
3. Continue to puree the mix until it is smooth.
4. Get a bowl, combine: 1/2 tsp salt and the eggs.
5. Whisk the eggs evenly then add in the carrot mix and hard boiled eggs.
6. Stir the mix again then add in the parsley.
7. Get your olive oil hot then begin to fry the egg mix for 5 mins then place everything under the broiler for 5 more mins.
8. Enjoy.

CLASSICAL
Lentils

Prep Time: 15 mins
Total Time: 6 h 15 mins

Servings per Recipe: 6
Calories   438.7
Cholesterol   0.0mg
Sodium   326.5mg
Carbohydrates   78.0g
Protein   26.3

Ingredients
2 large onions, diced
2 large carrots, peeled and diced
2 celery ribs, diced
1 tbsp oil
3 garlic cloves, finely chopped
1 1/2 C. green lentils
3 small red chilies
1 tsp harissa, see appendix

1 tsp ground cumin
2 can chopped tomatoes with juice
2 C. vegetable stock
2 cans red kidney beans, rinsed and drained
2 tbsps concentrated tomato paste
salt
ground black pepper

Directions
1. Begin to stir fry your carrots, onions, and celery, in oil for 10 mins then combine in the chili, garlic, harissa, and cumin.
2. Let the mix continue to cook for 60 secs then combine in the stock, lentils, tomato paste, and chopped tomatoes.
3. Get the mix boiling, set the heat to low, and let everything gently cook for 10 mins.
4. Now place the mix into the crock pot of a slow cooker and place a lid on the crock pot.
5. Let the content cook for 7 hrs with low level of heat.
6. When 1 hour is left of cooking time add in your kidney beans some pepper and salt.
7. Enjoy.

Harissa
Crab Bake

🥣 Prep Time: 40 mins
🕐 Total Time: 1 h 15 mins

Servings per Recipe: 8
Calories   533.6
Cholesterol   102.0mg
Sodium   1051.5mg
Carbohydrates   60.2g
Protein   32.7

Ingredients

1 1/2 lbs lump crabmeat, picked over
8 C. day-old white bread, cubes
3 C. warm water
3 tbsps butter
1 onion, diced small
1 red bell pepper, diced small
3 medium carrots, peeled and coarsely grated
3 garlic cloves, diced

1 tsp ground cumin
1 tsp dried oregano
1 tsp sweet paprika
salt and pepper
2 C. milk
1/4 C. heavy cream
1/2 C. vegetable broth
1 1/2 tbsps harissa, see appendix
2/3 C. fresh parmesan cheese, grated

Directions

1. Get a bowl, combine: water and the pieces of bread. Leave the mix for 30 mins.
2. Squeeze the bread together to remove all the liquids then break it into pieces.
3. Set your oven to 375 degrees before doing anything else.
4. Now get your butter hot and begin to stir fry your bell pepper and onions for 5 mins in the butter.
5. Now combine in the pepper, carrots, salt, cumin, garlic, paprika, and oregano.
6. Stir fry everything for 60 more secs then combine in the broth, bread, cream, and milk.
7. Continue to fry everything for 7 more mins then combine in the crab, stir the mix, then shut the heat.
8. Top everything with the harissa, some pepper and salt as well.
9. Then place the mix in a casserole dish.
10. Cover everything with the cheese and cook the dish in the oven for 22 mins.
11. Enjoy.

VEGETABLE, Chicken & Sausage Couscous

🥣 Prep Time: 45 mins
🕐 Total Time: 1 h 30 mins

Servings per Recipe: 6
Calories	934 kcal
Fat	39 g
Carbohydrates	80.5g
Protein	62.2 g
Cholesterol	169 mg
Sodium	601 mg

Ingredients

3 tbsp olive oil
2 lbs chicken thighs
12 oz. Italian turkey sausage
1 tbsp diced garlic
2 onions, minced
2 carrots, julienned
1/2 stalk celery, chunked
1 rutabaga, parsnip, or turnip, chunked
1/2 green bell pepper, julienned
1/2 red bell pepper, julienned
1 can diced tomatoes

1 can garbanzo beans
2 C. chicken stock
2 tsps thyme
1 tsp turmeric
1 tsp cayenne pepper
1/4 tsp harissa, see appendix
1 bay leaf
2 zucchini, cut in half
2 C. couscous
2 C. chicken stock
1/2 C. plain yogurt

Directions

1. Brown your chicken thighs all over in olive oil.
2. Add in your sausage and cook everything until fully done. Once it has cooled dice the sausage into pieces.
3. Now stir fry your garlic and onions until tender and see-through then combine in: stock, bay leaf, carrots, harissa, beans, celery, cayenne, tomatoes, turmeric, rutabaga, thyme, red and green peppers.
4. Cook for 2 more mins before adding your chicken and sausage.
5. Place a lid on the pan and cook for 35 mins until chicken is fully done.
6. Add your zucchini and cook for 7 more mins.
7. Meanwhile boil 2 C. of chicken stock then pour it over your couscous in a bowl along with 2 tbsps of olive oil.
8. Place a covering on the bowl and let it sit for at least 10 mins.
9. When plating the dish first layer couscous then some chicken mix and then some yogurt.
10. Enjoy.

Classical
North African Harissa

Prep Time: 20 mins
Total Time: 20 mins

Servings per Recipe: 40
Calories   28 kcal
Fat   2.8
Carbohydrates   0.9g
Protein   0.2 g
Cholesterol   0 mg
Sodium   176 mg

Ingredients

6 oz. bird's eye chilies, seeded and stems removed
12 cloves garlic, peeled
1 tbsp coriander, ground
1 tbsp ground cumin

1 tbsp salt
1 tbsp dried mint
1/2 C. chopped fresh cilantro
1/2 C. olive oil

Directions

1. Add the following to the bowl a food processor: chilies, cilantro, garlic, salt mint, coriander, and cumin.
2. Pulse the mix until it is smooth then add in some olive oil and pulse the mix a few more times.
3. Place the mix in jar and top everything with the rest of the oil.
4. Enjoy.

CLASSICAL
Tunisian Style Harissa

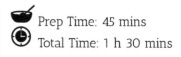 Prep Time: 45 mins
Total Time: 1 h 30 mins

Servings per Recipe: 192
Calories	10 kcal
Fat	0.3 g
Carbohydrates	1.9g
Protein	0.4 g
Cholesterol	0 mg
Sodium	26 mg

Ingredients
11 oz. dried red chili peppers, stems removed, seeds, removed
3/4 C. chopped garlic
2 C. caraway seed
1/2 tsp ground coriander seed
2 tsps salt

Directions
1. Let your chilies sit submerged in water for 30 mins then remove the liquids.
2. Now add the following to the bowl of a food processor: salt, pepper, coriander, garlic, and caraway.
3. Puree the mix then place everything into a Mason jar and top the mix with a bit of oil.
4. Place the lid on the jar tightly and put everything in the fridge.
5. Enjoy.

Classical
North African Harissa

Prep Time: 20 mins
Total Time: 20 mins

Servings per Recipe: 40
Calories	28 kcal
Fat	2.8
Carbohydrates	0.9g
Protein	0.2 g
Cholesterol	0 mg
Sodium	176 mg

Ingredients

6 oz. bird's eye chilies, seeded and stems removed
12 cloves garlic, peeled
1 tbsp coriander, ground
1 tbsp ground cumin

1 tbsp salt
1 tbsp dried mint
1/2 C. chopped fresh cilantro
1/2 C. olive oil

Directions

1. Add the following to the bowl a food processor: chilies, cilantro, garlic, salt mint, coriander, and cumin.
2. Pulse the mix until it is smooth then add in some olive oil and pulse the mix a few more times.
3. Place the mix in jar and top everything with the rest of the oil.
4. Enjoy.

Made in the USA
Monee, IL
19 December 2021

86431214R00033